BOOK ANALYSIS

Written by Laura Clements

Much Ado About Nothing

BY WILLIAM SHAKESPEARE

WILLIAM SHAKESPEARE

ENGLISH PLAYWRIGHT AND POET

- **Born in Stratford-upon-Avon in 1564.**
- **Died in Stratford-upon-Avon in 1616.**
- **Notable works:**
  - *The Winter's Tale* (1611), play
  - *A Midsummer Night's Dream* (1596), play
  - *The Taming of the Shrew* (c. 1590-1592), play

Shakespeare is best known as an English playwright who wrote highly influential comedies, tragedies, and history plays as well as sonnets and narrative poems. Shakespeare's works are studied and performed across the globe even today, and include his 154 sonnets as well as plays such as *Julius Caesar* (1599), and *King Lear* (c. 1603-1606). William was the son of John Shakespeare, a glove-maker from Stratford, and he married Anne Hathaway in his early adulthood with whom he had three children. As a boy, William attended Stratford's grammar school where he would have studied performance and rhetoric. Latin texts were on his school's core curriculum, meaning that Shakespeare would have studied writers such as Cicero, Seneca, Virgil, and his favourite poet Ovid. Such texts informed the plots and genres of his own plays, which gives an impression of how crucial Latin literature is to fully appreciating Shakespeare's works. As well as being a playwright, Shakespeare was also an actor, and it is speculated that he joined an acting company called the Queen's Men in Stratford-Upon-Avon.

MUCH ADO ABOUT NOTHING

THE COMIC TALE OF FOUR LOVERS

- **Genre:** romantic comedy play
- **Reference edition:** Shakespeare, W. (2018) *Much Ado About Nothing*. Cambridge: Cambridge University Press.
- **1st edition:** (c. 1598-1599)
- **Themes:** female chastity, vengeance, male jealousy, disguise, reconciliation, appearances

Much Ado About Nothing is said to be the most popular of Shakespeare's comedies, and is still regularly performed today. The play follows the usual Shakespearean comedy format which revolves around a misunderstanding that is eventually resolved and ends happily for the characters involved. This stylistic technique is an inversion of Shakespeare's tragedy plots in which miscommunications are not resolved until it is too late, such as in *Romeo and Juliet* (c. 1594-1596). *Much Ado About Nothing* differs stylistically from Shakespeare's other plays since the main plot is written in verse whilst the sub-plot is in prose. There is no definitive explanation as to why this is, but it could be to distinguish the importance of the main plot from the supporting narrative, which is more carefree in nature. Stanley Wells and Gary Taylor identify the plot's main device, which sees Claudio tricked into believing that his lover has been unfaithful, as "a variation on an old tale that existed in many versions" (1987: 661) by writers such as Ludovico Ariosto (Italian poet, 1474-1533) in his *Orlando Furioso* (1516) and Matteo Bandello (Italian writer and bishop, c. 1480-1562) in his *Novelle* (1554). The unveiling of the plot and reconciliation of the lovers at the end of the play makes *Much Ado About Nothing* one of the best early modern examples of "tragicomical resolution" (*ibid.*).

SUMMARY

FOUR LOVERS MEET

The play is set in the Italian town of Messina, where Don Pedro, the Prince of Aragon, returns home after the war with his friends Benedick and Claudio, and his bitter half-brother Don John. He visits Leonato, the Duke of Messina, in his home. Claudio and Hero, Leonato's daughter, fall in love immediately when they meet in Leonato's house, and Don Pedro makes arrangements for them to be married.

Benedick and Beatrice have a verbal sparring match whenever they meet, yet also joke with one another about their disregard for romantic love. In one of her first quips toward Benedick, Beatrice responds to him by saying "I wonder that you will still be talking, Signor Benedick, / nobody marks you" (1.1.86-87), and Benedick responds by calling her his "dear Lady Disdain" (1.1.88). This conversation sets the tone for their relationship prior to Don Pedro and their friends' plot to make Benedick and Beatrice fall in love with each other. During the week leading up to Claudio and Hero's wedding, their friends plan for Benedick and Beatrice to overhear conversations about their love for one another. Their attempts are successful, and Benedick and Beatrice secretly fall in love with each other.

CLAUDIO IS DECEIVED

Don Pedro's reclusive and unfriendly half-brother Don John fabricates a malicious plot with his follower Borachio to ruin Claudio's marriage to Hero. The plot leads Claudio to believe that Hero has committed adultery the night before their wedding day, when in actual fact he saw Hero's maid Margaret with Borachio.

Claudio confronts Hero about her infidelity during their marriage ceremony and slanders her in front of her family and friends, which causes her to faint; Claudio then abandons her at the altar. Claudio asks the wedding congregation, "Would you not swear / All you that see her, that she were a maid, / By these exterior shows? But she is none: / She knows the heat of a luxurious bed" (4.1.33-36). Despite this onslaught of public insults, the Friar believes Hero to be innocent and tells her family to announce that she has died of shock, and keep her safe until news of her innocence is revealed. The Friar tells the family to "Let her awhile be secretly kept in, / And publish it, that she is dead indeed: Maintain a mourning ostentation, / And on your family's old monument / Hang mournful epitaphs, and do all rites, / That appertain unto a burial" (4.1.196-201).

BEATRICE AND BENEDICK COME TOGETHER

Amongst all the heartache, Benedick and Beatrice confess their love for one another. Benedick tells his lover to "Come bid me do anything for thee" (4.1.278) to which she immediately replies "Kill Claudio" (4.1.279). Beatrice's request is intended to revenge Claudio's treatment of Hero at the altar, and she exploits Benedick's promise to achieve this end. It is Beatrice's gender that prevents her from avenging Hero for herself, and she states to Benedick several times in the following speeches "Oh God that I were a man! I would eat his heart in the market place" (4.1.294-295).

THE PLOT IS UNCOVERED

Before there is time for the duel between Benedick and Claudio to take place, Don John's plot is exposed when the constables Dogberry and Verges overhear Borachio bragging about his evening with Margaret (supposed by Claudio to have been Hero). Borachio and Conrade are arrested and interrogated. It is during this interrogation scene that the audience comes to realise how gullible and foolish Dogberry is. The constable takes the words of the criminals at face value: upon stating that Conrade and Borachio are "false knaves" (4.2.24) Borachio immediately responds that "we are none" (4.2.25). This proclamation appears to be enough for Dogberry, who asks Sexton "have you writ down, that they are none?" (4.2.27), to which Sexton reminds him that "you go not the way to examine, you must call forth the watch that are their accusers" (4.2.28-29). Having such a dim-witted character save the characters from further suffering adds to the satire of the play. When news of the plot reaches Claudio, he realises that Hero was innocent and grieves her death. Leonato tells Claudio that he must tell everyone in the town of Hero's innocence, and asks him to marry his niece Beatrice in the place of the 'dead' Hero. However, at the marriage ceremony Beatrice is unmasked and is revealed to be Hero after all, and Claudio is filled with joy. When Hero is unmasked, Leonato states that "She died, my lord, but whiles her slander lived" (5.4.66). This line is crucial in understanding how, in *Much Ado About Nothing*, a woman's worth is synonymous with her sexual integrity. News is also revealed that Don John has been permanently imprisoned.

A JOINT WEDDING

During the reconciliation scene, Benedick also goes back on his prior distaste towards marriage and asks Beatrice to marry him, to which she agrees. Benedick states to Don Pedro, "I do propose to marry [...] and therefore never flout at me, for what I have said against it: for man is a giddy thing, and this is my conclusion" (5.4.101-104). The play ends in a celebratory dance as the two couples prepare for their joint wedding.

CHARACTER STUDY

CLAUDIO

Claudio is a young nobleman who served in Don Pedro's army and falls in love with Hero. Claudio is easily manipulated by his commander's half-brother Don John into believing that his fiancé has been unfaithful to him. It is exactly this gullibility that drives the plot of the play. Claudio apologises when he finds out that Hero was actually innocent, stating, "yet sinned I not, / But in mistaking" (5.1.241-242). Claudio's acknowledgment of his misjudgement is rather flippant and he does not try hard to show any remorse for Hero's sake. However, Leonato ensures that Claudio tells the town of Hero's innocence.

HERO

Hero is the heroine of the play who meets Claudio when he arrives home from the war and immediately falls in love with him when he visits her father's house. Hero is falsely accused of committing adultery, and is shamed at the altar despite her innocence. Hero's supposed death drives Claudio to make a public declaration of her innocence and sets up the revelation at the close of the play when she appears back at the altar disguised as her cousin. Despite being a central protagonist, Hero has very little agency in the play and often has her identity constructed by people's perceptions of her supposed actions.

LEONATO

A respected nobleman and Governor who is father to Hero and uncle to Beatrice. Leonato welcomes Don Pedro and his men into his home after the war, and later requests that Claudio marry his 'niece' after Hero reportedly dies of shame at the altar.

BEATRICE

Beatrice wants vengeance on the man who has besmirched her cousin's honour. However, Travis D. Williams argues that she takes her anger towards the situation too far. He states that "Beatrice's anger is the anger of impotence, but it is also embarrassing if stretched too much" (2018: 42). Beatrice is completely set against marriage at the beginning of the play; when her uncle tells her that one day he hopes to see her married, she responds that "Adam's sons are my brethren, and truly I hold it a sin to match in my kindred" (2.1.46-47). Beatrice also does not believe she could be faithful in marriage, as when Leonato tells her that "God will send you no horns" (2.1.20), she responds "Just, if he send me no husband" (2.1.21). This is just one of many cuckold jokes made in the play, and reflects Beatrice's unwillingness to become a dedicated wife.

BENEDICK

Benedick is the other component in the sub-plot, one of Don Pedro's men who falls in love with Beatrice as a consequence of his friends' match-making. Williams argues that when Benedick gives himself to Beatrice, his role changes and he must step away from his prior identity as Claudio's ally and become the "courtly servant-lover", since "as a gentleman of honour who has made the offer of his love to a lady with the intention of marriage, the honour of her family becomes his responsibility, and by this route also he is obliged to challenge Claudio" (2018: 40). As such, falling in love with Beatrice changes his characterisation and his purpose in the play, as he must turn against Claudio to prove his loyalty to his future wife and her family. Despite being the sub-plot, the relationship between Benedick and Beatrice is as fundamental to the play as Claudio and Hero's romance. This is supported by Wells and Taylor, who argue that "although Benedick and Beatrice are, technically, subordinate characters, they have dominated the imagination of both readers and playgoers" (1987: 661).

DON PEDRO

Don Pedro is the Prince of Aragon and half-brother to the bitter Don John whom he just returned from defeating at war. When the brothers reconcile they return to Leonato's house in Messina. It is Don Pedro who encourages the marriage between Claudio and Hero and also who initiates the match-making plan between Hero and Claudio. As such, it is Don Pedro who sets up the events that drive the plot.

DON JOHN

The illegitimate half-brother of Don Pedro, Don John is a bitter and malicious character whose motivation is to prevent the marriage of his brother Claudio to Hero. He proclaims to Conrade that "I am a plain-dealing villain" (1.3.23-24), and when Borachio informs him of the wedding plans he asks, "will it serve for any model to build mischief on?" (1.3.34). Don John evidently makes other characters uncomfortable with his temperament, for instance Beatrice tells Leonato that "I never can see him but I am heart-burned an hour after" (2.1.3-4). Despite his cold actions, Emma Smith (2012) argues that Don John's transparency about his character distinguishes him from other characters in this play who try to veil their true selves.

BORACHIO AND CONRADE

Followers of Don John who assist him in making Claudio believe that Hero has been unfaithful to him. They are arrested and imprisoned when their plot is exposed by police constable Dogberry.

MARGARET

Margaret is Hero's maid and is used as part of the plot to make Claudio believe that Hero has been unfaithful. However, her part in the plan is forgiven during the reconciliation when Leonato states that "Margaret was in some fault for this, / Although against her will as it appears" (5.4.4-5). Margaret's lover is Borachio, and she unintentionally finds herself tied to the scheming and unlawful side of the plot.

DOGBERRY

A comical watchman who facilitates the happy ending of the play. Dogberry is a member of the police force who uncovers the plot by Don John to break up the marriage of Hero and Claudio. Despite being a member of the Italian police, Dogberry is dim-witted and often confuses his words. Williams argues that Dogberry has particular struggles with his uses of language, since he, "with sublime nonchalance, says usually the opposite of what he means, or, where he does achieve his own meaning – 'O that I had been writ down an ass' – it is one that can be subverted by the hearers" (2018: 38). Williams elaborates that in this sense, Dogberry fits with the importance of the misinterpretation of words more widely in the play.

ANALYSIS

APPEARANCES

The way that characters appear to one another and to the audience is also central to driving the plot. Williams makes the following argument about the play's use of clothes as a prop:

> "[They are] an important visual element in the play. We should assume a shift from the martial to the lover-like in Claudio and later Benedick; there are the disguises of the mask, the finery and vestments of the wedding, mourning clothes for the scene at Hero's monument, and a final change to 'other weeds' for the last scene." (2018: 39)

Williams' argument demonstrates how characters and their actions are often taken at face value in the play. In addition, when Leonato is discussing the idea of Beatrice taking a husband without a beard, she responds, "What should I do with him – dress him in my apparel and make him my waiting gentlewoman?" (2.1.25-

26). This scene focuses on the appearances of husbands, and the idea that a man without facial hair would be too young a match for Beatrice, while she could not endure one with a beard, for "I had rather lie in the woollen!" (2.1.23-24). Beatrice's prejudices towards men both with and without beards not only expresses her distaste towards marriage but also demonstrates how identity is inseparable from outward appearances for Shakespeare's characters. Ideas of appearance are also related to the mask performance which takes part in Act Two. The mask was a form of entertainment both in the home and at court in Elizabethan England. Williams identifies that "the quarto of *Much Ado* does not indicate a mask, though it is clear from the dialogue that this is what takes place" (2018: 169). The original stage directions read "*Enter* DON PEDRO, CLAUDIO, BENEDICK *and* BALTHASAR, *Maskers with a drum* [...] *The dance begins*" (2.1.60). This mask entertainment, which would have included members of the audience, relates to the idea of characters choosing to hide their true identities.

SPEECH

Speeches drive the plot of *Much Ado About Nothing*. It is the interpretation (or misinterpretation) of speech that determines the breakdowns and, later, successes of the two romance narratives. Maurice Hunt makes the following argument:

> "[L]ove arises when stratagems of eavesdropping make Benedick, Beatrice, and Claudio fall either in or out of love, but they do so only because of what other characters say, only because of the speech uttered and the attitude of members of the trio toward it." (2000: 116)

Hunt's idea that romantic love is fabricated through the interpretation of speech in this play demonstrates how the spoken word is a central plot driver since it has the capacity to awaken or establish feelings in the Shakespeare's characters. Hunt elaborates that "Shakespeare unforgettably invites the question of the relation of spoken language to the truth by showing how easily the words of others cause Benedick and Beatrice to fall in and out of love" (*ibid*.). Therefore, speech is the most significant plot driver in the play since characters trust one another's words to the extent that it shapes their personal choices and the subsequent outcomes. The very power that speeches hold in *Much Ado* illustrates how easily manipulated the characters truly are.

FEMALE SEXUALITY

The play is rife with allusions to cuckoldry, especially in relation to Beatrice and Hero. Male characters constantly obsess over the idea of controlling female sexuality through marriage. Ian Innes has identified the significance of the pun 'nothing' in the title *Much Ado About Nothing,* basing his analysis on the definition by Claire McEachern's gloss that "*nothing* was slang for the female genitalia, and was pronounced the same way as 'noting', which could mean 'noticing' or 'knowing'" (2005: 2). Innes argues that "it condenses an awareness of the play as not being about much that matters, as being very much concerned with the woman's place, and also being a very self-aware dramatic artefact, one that is intimately concerned with the process of representation as noting/knowing" (2014: 1-2).

Female sexuality is at the centre of the play; however, Hero is proven faithful at the end of the play whilst Beatrice's potentially threatening sexuality is neutralised by her engagement to Benedick. In this light, it is interesting to compare it with other Shakespearean plays that scrutinise female sexuality, such as the tragedy of *Othello* (1604) that ends with Desdemona's death when news of her innocence comes too late.

MALE RELATIONSHIPS

In a play that appears so deeply concerned with the romantic relationships between men and women, *Much Ado About Nothing* is perhaps more interested in homosocial dynamics. Emma Smith (2012) argues that this play is about male relationships, not about the relationships between men and women as the romantic comedy genre may lead us to believe. She argues that the un-doing of the heterosexual relationship asserts masculine bonds in the play. This also suggests that Hero has very little agency, as she is rendered disloyal by an unclear image through a window. Smith uses the example of when Don Pedro tells Claudio that he will woo Hero on his behalf, which demonstrates how the play substitutes male relationships with male-female ones. She elaborates that this relationship between Hero and Claudio is made to cement the bond between the men who set up the marriage (namely Leonato, Don Pedro, and Claudio), whilst Hero has no agency or choice in the matter. Building on Smith's idea, one may consider how female agency is limited in the play whilst the male characters obsess over ideas of female sexuality and marriage in order to establish control over women and bonds with one another.

TWO WEDDINGS OR NONE?

Despite the fact that *Much Ado About Nothing* is primarily concerned with who will marry whom, it is curious that the much-anticipated wedding is not included in the action. This idea has been researched by Nathanial Leonard (2017), who has identified that in Shakespearean comedies neither wedding ceremonies nor the legalities of marriage are ever acted onstage. Leonard argues that "although the absence of staged religious marriage ceremonies is easily justified by Queen

Elizabeth I's effective ban on the staging of religious subject matter [...] the ban does not explain why legal marriage rites are set up by the plots of Shakespeare's comedies only to be avoided and undermined" (2017: 303). In short, Leonard answers this absence by showing how staging an early modern marriage was taboo since it was theologically and financially complex, leading Shakespeare to use "the deferment of early modern marriage rites as the catalyst for comic closure" (*ibid*.). The absence of a wedding in a play about marriage allowed Shakespeare to avoid treading on delicate ground whilst also creating comic closure through the substitute dance at the end of the play. Therefore, the audience feel as though they have been part of the marriage ritual without ever actually experiencing it.

FURTHER REFLECTION

SOME QUESTIONS TO THINK ABOUT...

- Does the play's sub-plot (the relationship between Benedick and Beatrice) add anything to our understanding of the main plot?
- How might the ending of the play be changed if *Much Ado* was a tragedy?
- Do you think that Claudio's reaction to Hero's supposed infidelity was too extreme or completely justified?
- What is the significance of disguise in the play and how does it help to drive the plot?
- Why do you think that Don John is bitter in the play, and what are his motivations for preventing the marriage?
- How is speech affected by gender in the play?
- What is your take on the power dynamics in the romantic pairings? Do the male or female characters hold more sway?
- Why do you think that Shakespeare chose to set this play in Italy? Would the action change if it was set in England?

- Which pair do you think dominates the play: Hero and Claudio, or Benedick and Beatrice?
- Why do you think the characters trust Don John enough to let his plot take off?

We want to hear from you!
Leave a comment on your online library
and share your favourite books on social media!

FURTHER READING

REFERENCE EDITION

- Shakespeare, W. (2018) *Much Ado About Nothing*. Cambridge: Cambridge University Press.

REFERENCE STUDIES

- Holland, P. (2013) Shakespeare, William. *The Oxford Dictionary of National Biography*. [Online]. [Accessed 19 October 2018]. Available from: <https://doi.org/10.1093/ref:odnb/25200>

- Hunt, M. (2000) The Reclamation of Language in "Much Ado about Nothing". *Studies in Philology*. 97(2), pp. 165-191.

- Innes, I. (2014) Sensory Confusion and the Generation Gap in *Much Ado About Nothing*. *Critical Survey*. 26(2), pp. 1-20.

- Leonard, N. C. (2017) Circling the Nuptial in *As You Like It* and *Much Ado about Nothing*. *Studies in English Literature 1500-1900*. 57(2), pp. 303-323.

- (No date) Much Ado About Nothing. *Royal Shakespeare Company*. [Online resources]. [Accessed 28 November 2018]. Available from: <https://www.rsc.org.uk/

much-ado-about-nothing>

- Shakespeare, W. (2005) *Much Ado About Nothing*. Ed. McEachern, C. Bloomsbury: The Arden Shakespeare.

- Smith, E. (2012) Much Ado About Nothing. *Approaching Shakespeare*. [Podcast]. [Accessed 28 November 2018]. Available from: <https:// podcasts.ox.ac.uk/much-ado-about-nothing>

- Wells, S. and Taylor, G. (1987) Introduction. *The Complete Oxford Shakespeare, vol. 2.* Oxford: Oxford University Press.

- Williams, T. D. (2018) Introduction to Shakespeare, W. *Much Ado About Nothing.* Cambridge: Cambridge University Press.

ADAPTATIONS

- *Love's Labour's Won,* or *Much Ado About Nothing* (2014) [Play]. Christopher Luscombe. Dir. UK: RSC.

- *Much Ado About Nothing* (1993) [Film]. Kenneth Branagh. Dir. UK: BBC Films.

MORE FROM BRIGHTSUMMARIES.COM

- Reading guide – *Antony and Cleopatra* by William Shakespeare.

- Reading guide – *Hamlet* by William Shakespeare.

- Reading guide – *Julius Caesar* by William Shakespeare.

- Reading guide – *King Lear* by William Shakespeare.

- Reading guide – *Macbeth* by William Shakespeare.

- Reading guide – *Measure for Measure* by William Shakespeare.

- Reading guide – *The Merchant of Venice* by William Shakespeare.

- Reading guide – *A Midsummer Night's Dream* by William Shakespeare.

- Reading guide – *Othello* by William Shakespeare.

- Reading guide – *Richard III* by William Shakespeare.

- Reading guide – *Romeo and Juliet* by William Shakespeare.

- Reading guide – *The Tempest* by William Shakespeare.

- Reading guide – *Titus Andronicus* by William Shakespeare.

- Reading guide – *Twelfth Night* by William Shakespeare.

- Reading guide – *The Two Gentlemen of Verona* by William Shakespeare.

www.brightsummaries.com

Ebook EAN: 9782808016018

Paperback EAN: 9782808016025

Legal Deposit: D/2018/12603/561

Cover: © Primento

Digital conception by Primento, the digital partner of
publishers.